Translated by

AUGUSTA WEBSTER

First published in 1868

Published by Read & Co. Books,
an imprint of Read & Co.

The Medea of Euripides first published in 1868.
This edition published by Read & Co. in 2024

Extra material © 2024 Read & Co. Books

All rights reserved. No portion of this book may be reproduced in any form without the permission of the publisher in writing.

A catalogue record for this book is available from the British Library.

ISBN: 9781528724036

Read & Co. is part of Read Books Ltd.
For more information visit www.readandcobooks.co.uk

CONTENTS

AUGUSTA WEBSTER
A Biography.. 5
AN INTRODUCTION TO THE MEDEA OF EURIPIDES
By Gilbert Murray.................................... 11
CHARACTERS OF THE PLAY......................... 17
MEDEA 19
MEDEA IN ATHENS
Augusta Webster, *Portraits*, 1870 93

AUGUSTA WEBSTER

1837–1894

WEBSTER, Mrs. AUGUSTA, poet, was born at Poole, Dorset, on 30 Jan. 1837 (her full christian names were Julia Augusta). Her father, Vice-admiral George Davies (1800–1876), attained great distinction for services in saving lives from shipwreck (O'Byrne, *Naval Biography*, pp. 266–7). Her mother, Julia (1803–1897), was the fourth daughter of Joseph Hume (1767–1843) of Somerset House, the intimate friend and associate of Lamb, Hazlitt, and Godwin. Hume was of mixed English, Scottish, and French extraction, and claimed descent from the Humes of Polwarth. He was the author of a translation in blank verse of Dante's 'Inferno' (1812) and of 'A Search into the Old Testament' (1841).

Augusta's earliest years were spent on board the Griper in Chichester Harbour and at various seaside places where her father, as lieutenant in the coastguard, held command. In 1842 he attained the rank of commander, and was appointed the next year to the Banff district. The family resided for six years in Banff Castle, and Augusta attended a school at Banff. After a short period spent at Penzance, Davies was appointed in 1851 chief constable of Cambridgeshire, and settled with his family in Cambridge. In 1857 he was nominated also to the chief constableship of Huntingdonshire. At Cambridge Augusta read widely, and attended classes at the Cambridge school of art. During a brief residence at Paris and Geneva she acquired a full knowledge of French. She studied Greek in order to help a young brother, and subsequently learned Italian and Spanish.

In 1860 she published, under the name of Cecil Home, a volume entitled 'Blanche Lisle, and other Poems.' Under the same pseudonym appeared in 1864 'Lilian Gray,' a poem, and 'Lesley's Guardians,' a novel in three volumes.

In December 1863 Augusta Davies married Mr. Thomas Webster, then fellow, and afterwards law lecturer, of Trinity College, Cambridge. There was one child of the marriage, a daughter. In 1870 they left Cambridge for London, where Mr. Webster practised his profession. Meanwhile Mrs. Webster published in 1866 a literal translation into English verse of 'The Prometheus Bound' of Æschylus. This, and all her subsequent publications, appeared under her own name. She was not a Greek scholar, but her translations—in 1868 appeared the 'Medea' of Euripides—obtained praise from scholars, and proved her a sympathetic student of Greek literature. Her views on translation may be found in two excellent essays contributed to the 'Examiner,' entitled 'The Translation of Poetry' and 'A Transcript and a Transcription' (cf. A Housewife's Opinions, pp. 61-79). The latter is a review of Browning's 'Agamemnon.' Mrs. Webster's first important volume of original verse, 'Dramatic Studies,' was published in 1866. It contains 'The Snow-waste,' one of her best poems. In 1870 appeared 'Portraits,' Mrs. Webster's most striking work in verse apart from her dramas. It reached a second edition in the year of publication, and a third in 1893. A remarkable poem, 'The Castaway,' won the admiration of Browning, and deserves a place by the side of Rossetti's 'Jenny.' Her first effort in the poetic drama was 'The Auspicious Day,' published in 1872. It is a romance of mediæval English life of small interest. 'Disguises,' written in 1879, is a play of great charm, containing beautiful lyrics.

Mrs. Webster took as keen an interest in the practical affairs of life as in literature. In 1878 appeared 'A Housewife's

Opinions,' a volume of essays on various social subjects, reprinted from the 'Examiner.' She served twice on the London school board. In November 1879 she was returned for the Chelsea division at the head of the poll, with 3,912 votes above the second successful candidate; she owed her success to her gift of speech. She threw herself heart and soul into the work. Mrs. Webster was a working rather than a talking member of the board. She was anxious to popularise education by bringing old endowments into closer contact with elementary schools, and she anticipated the demand that, as education is a national necessity, it should also be a national charge. She advocated the introduction of technical (i.e. manual) instruction into elementary schools. Her leanings were frankly democratic, but in the heat of controversy her personality rendered her attractive even to her most vigorous opponents. In consequence of ill-health, which obliged her to seek rest in the south of Europe, she did not offer herself for re-election in 1882.

During earlier visits to Italy Mrs. Webster had been attracted by the Italian peasant songs known as 'rispetti,' and in 1881 published 'A Book of Rhyme,' containing rural poems called 'English rispetti.' She was the first to introduce the form into English poetry. In 1882 she published another drama, 'In a Day,' the only one of her plays that was acted. It was produced at a matinée at Terry's Theatre, London, in 1890, when her daughter, Miss Davies Webster, played the heroine, Klydone. It had a *succès d'estime*. In 1885 she was again returned member of the school board for Chelsea. She conducted her candidature without a committee or any organised canvassing.

'The Sentence,' a three-act tragedy, in many ways Mrs. Webster's chief work, appeared in 1887. The episode of which the play treats illustrates Caligula's revengeful spirit (cf. Rossetti's introductory note to Mrs. Webster's *Mother and Daughter*, pp. 12-14). It was much admired by Christina

Rossetti (cf. Mackenzie Bell's *Christina Rossetti*, p. 161). A volume of selections from Mrs. Webster's poems (containing some originally contributed to magazines), published in 1893, was well received. She died at Kew on 5 Sept. 1894. In 1895 appeared 'Mother and Daughter,' an uncompleted sonnet-sequence, with an introductory note by Mr. William Michael Rossetti.

A half-length portrait in crayons by Canevari, drawn at Rome in January 1864, is in the possession of Mr. Webster.

Mrs. Webster's verse entitles her to a high place among English poets. She used with success the form of the dramatic monologue. She often sacrificed beauty to strength, but she possessed much metrical skill and an ear for melody. Some of her lyrics deserve a place in every anthology of modern English poetry. Many of her poems treat entirely or incidentally of questions specially affecting women. She was a warm advocate of woman's suffrage—her essays in the 'Examiner' on the subject were reprinted as leaflets by the Women's Suffrage Society (cf. Mackenzie Bell's *Life of Christina Rossetti*, p. 111)—and she sympathised with all movements in favour of a better education for women.

Works by Augusta Webster, not mentioned in the text, are:
1. 'A Woman Sold, and other Poems,' 1867.
2. 'Yu-Pe-Ya's Lute: a Chinese Tale in English Verse,' 1874.
3. 'Daffodil and the Croäxaxicans: a Romance of History,' 1884.

A selection from her poems is given in Miles's 'Poets and Poetry of the Century' (Joanna Baillie to Mathilde Blind, p. 499).

—Elizabeth Lee,
Dictionary of National Biography,
1885-1900, Volume 60

THE MEDEA OF EURIPIDES
Literally Translated into English Verse

Translated by

AUGUSTA WEBSTER

With an Introduction by

GILBERT MURRAY

AN INTRODUCTION TO THE MEDEA OF EURIPIDES

By Gilbert Murray

The *Medea*, in spite of its background of wonder and enchantment, is not a romantic play but a tragedy of character and situation. It deals, so to speak, not with the romance itself, but with the end of the romance, a thing which is so terribly often the reverse of romantic. For all but the very highest of romances are apt to have just one flaw somewhere, and in the story of Jason and Medea the flaw was of a fatal kind.

The wildness and beauty of the Argo legend run through all Greek literature, from the mass of Corinthian lays older than our present Iliad, which later writers vaguely associate with the name of Eumêlus, to the Fourth Pythian Ode of Pindar and the beautiful Argonautica of Apollonius Rhodius. Our poet knows the wildness and the beauty; but it is not these qualities that he specially seeks. He takes them almost for granted, and pierces through them to the sheer tragedy that lies below.

Jason, son of Aeson, King of Iôlcos, in Thessaly, began his life in exile. His uncle Pelias had seized his father's kingdom, and Jason was borne away to the mountains by night and given, wrapped in a purple robe, to Chiron, the Centaur. When he reached manhood he came down to Iôlcos to demand, as Pindar tells us, his ancestral honour, and stood in the market-place, a world-famous figure, one-sandalled, with his pard-skin, his two spears and his long hair, gentle and wild and fearless, as the Wise Beast had reared him. Pelias, cowed but loath to yield, promised to give up the kingdom if Jason would make his way to the unknown land of Colchis and perform a double quest. First, if I read Pindar aright, he must fetch back the soul of his kinsman Phrixus, who had died there far from home; and, secondly, find the fleece of the Golden Ram which Phrixus had sacrificed. Jason undertook the quest: gathered the most daring heroes from all parts of Hellas; built the first ship, Argo, and set to sea. After all manner of desperate adventures he reached the land of Aiêtês, king of the Colchians, and there hope failed him. By policy, by tact, by sheer courage he did all that man could do. But Aiêtês was both hostile and treacherous. The Argonauts were surrounded, and their destruction seemed only a question of days when, suddenly, unasked, and by the mercy of Heaven, Aiêtês' daughter, Mêdêa, an enchantress as well as a princess, fell in love with Jason. She helped him through all his trials; slew for him her own sleepless serpent, who guarded the fleece; deceived her father, and secured both the fleece and the soul of Phrixus. At the last moment it appeared that her brother, Absyrtus, was about to lay an ambush for Jason. She invited Absyrtus to her room, stabbed him dead, and fled with Jason over the seas. She had given up all, and expected in return a perfect love.

And what of Jason? He could not possibly avoid taking Medea with him. He probably rather loved her. She formed at the least a brilliant addition to the glory of his enterprise. Not many heroes could produce a barbarian princess ready to leave all and follow them in blind trust. For of course, as every one knew without the telling in fifth-century Athens, no legal marriage was possible between a Greek and a barbarian from Colchis.

All through the voyage home, a world-wide baffled voyage by the Ister and the Eridanus and the African Syrtes,

Medea was still in her element, and proved a constant help and counsellor to the Argonauts. When they reached Jason's home, where Pelias was still king, things began to be different. An ordered and law-abiding Greek state was scarcely the place for the untamed Colchian. We only know the catastrophe. She saw with smothered rage how Pelias hated Jason and was bent on keeping the kingdom from him, and she determined to do her lover another act of splendid service. Making the most of her fame as an enchantress, she persuaded Pelias that he could, by a certain process, regain his youth. He eagerly caught at the hope. His daughters tried the process upon him, and Pelias died in agony. Surely Jason would be grateful now!

The real result was what it was sure to be in a civilised country. Medea and her lover had to fly for their lives, and Jason was debarred for ever from succeeding to the throne of Iôlcos. Probably there was another result also in Jason's mind: the conclusion that at all costs he must somehow separate himself from this wild beast of a woman who was ruining his life. He directed their flight to Corinth, governed at the time by a ruler of some sort, whether "tyrant" or king, who was growing old and had an only daughter. Creon would naturally want a son-in-law to support and succeed him. And where in all Greece could he find one stronger or more famous than the chief of the Argonauts? If only Medea were not there! No doubt Jason owed her a great debt for her various services. Still, after all, he was not married to her. And a man must not be weak in such matters as these. Jason accepted the princess's hand, and when Medea became violent, found it difficult to be really angry with Creon for instantly condemning her to exile. At this point the tragedy begins.

The *Medea* is one of the earliest of Euripides' works now preserved to us. And those of us who have in our time glowed at all with the religion of realism, will probably feel in it many of the qualities of youth. Not, of course, the more normal, sensuous, romantic youth, the youth of *Romeo and Juliet*; but another kind—crude, austere, passionate—the youth of the poet who is also a sceptic and a devotee of truth, who so hates the conventionally and falsely beautiful that he is apt to be unduly ascetic towards beauty itself. When a writer really deficient in poetry walks in this path, the result is purely disagreeable. It produces its best results when the writer, like Euripides or Tolstoy, is so possessed by an inward flame of poetry that it breaks out at the great moments and consumes the cramping theory that would hold it in. One can feel in the Medea that the natural and inevitable romance of the story is kept rigidly down. One word about Medea's ancient serpent, two or three references to the Clashing Rocks, one startling flash of light upon the real love of Jason's life, love for the ship Argo, these are almost all the concessions made to us by the merciless delineator of disaster into whose hands we are fallen. Jason is a middle-aged man, with much glory, indeed, and some illusions; but a man entirely set upon building up a great career, to whom love and all its works, though at times he has found them convenient, are for the most part only irrational and disturbing elements in a world which he can otherwise mould to his will. And yet, most cruel touch of all, one feels this man to be the real Jason. It is not that he has fallen from his heroic past. It is that he was really like this always. And so with Medea. It is not only that her beauty has begun to fade; not only that she is set in surroundings which vaguely belittle and weaken her, making her no more a bountiful princess, but only an ambiguous and much criticised foreigner. Her very devotion of love for Jason, now turned to hatred, shows itself to have been always of that somewhat rank and ugly sort to which such a change is natural.

For concentrated dramatic quality and sheer intensity of passion few plays ever written can vie with the *Medea*. Yet it obtained only a third prize at its first production; and, in spite of its immense fame, there are not many scholars who would put it among their favourite tragedies. The comparative failure of the first production was perhaps due chiefly to the extreme originality of the play. The Athenians in 432 B.C. had not yet learnt to understand or tolerate such work as this, though it is likely enough that they fortified their unfavourable opinion by the sort of criticisms which we still find attributed to Aristotle and Dicæarchus.

At the present time it is certainly not the newness of the subject: I do not think it is Aegeus, nor yet the dragon chariot, much less Medea's involuntary burst of tears in the second scene with Jason, that really produces the feeling of dissatisfaction with which many people must rise from this great play. It is rather the general scheme on which the drama is built. It is a scheme which occurs again and again in Euripides, a study of oppression and revenge. Such a subject in the hands of a more ordinary writer would probably take the form of a triumph of oppressed virtue. But Euripides gives us nothing so sympathetic, nothing so cheap and unreal. If oppression usually made people virtuous, the problems of the world would be very different from what they are. Euripides seems at times to hate the revenge of the oppressed almost as much as the original cruelty of the oppressor; or, to put the same fact in a different light, he seems deliberately to dwell upon the twofold evil of cruelty, that it not only causes pain to the victim, but actually by means of the pain makes him a worse man, so that when his turn of triumph comes, it is no longer a triumph of justice or a thing to make men rejoice. This is a grim lesson; taught often enough by history, though seldom by the fables of the poets.

Seventeen years later than the *Medea* Euripides expressed this sentiment in a more positive way in the *Trojan Women*, where a depth of wrong borne without revenge becomes, or seems for the moment to become, a thing beautiful and glorious. But more plays are constructed like the *Medea*. The

Hecuba begins with a noble and injured Queen, and ends with her hideous vengeance on her enemy and his innocent sons. In the Orestes all our hearts go out to the suffering and deserted prince, till we find at last that we have committed ourselves to the blood-thirst of a madman. In the *Electra*, the workers of the vengeance themselves repent.

The dramatic effect of this kind of tragedy is curious. No one can call it undramatic or tame. Yet it is painfully unsatisfying. At the close of the *Medea* I actually find myself longing for a *deus ex machinâ*, for some being like Artemis in the *Hippolytus* or the good Dioscuri of the *Electra*, to speak a word of explanation or forgiveness, or at least leave some sound of music in our ears to drown that dreadful and insistent clamour of hate. The truth is that in this play Medea herself is the *dea ex machinâ*. The woman whom Jason and Creon intended simply to crush has been transformed by her injuries from an individual human being into a sort of living Curse. She is inspired with superhuman force. Her wrongs and her hate fill all the sky. And the judgment pronounced on Jason comes not from any disinterested or peace-making God, but from his own victim transfigured into a devil.

From any such judgment there is an instant appeal to sane human sympathy. Jason has suffered more than enough. But that also is the way of the world. And the last word upon these tragic things is most often something not to be expressed by the sentences of even the wisest articulate judge, but only by the unspoken *lacrimæ rerum*.

—GILBERT MURRAY,
Medea of Euripides, 1912

CHARACTERS OF THE PLAY

MEDEA, *daughter of Aiêtês, King of Colchis.*

JASON, *chief of the Argonauts; nephew of Pelias, King of Iôlcos in Thessaly.*

CREON, *ruler of Corinth.*

AEGEUS, *King of Athens.*

NURSE *of Medea.*

TWO CHILDREN *of Jason and Medea.*

ATTENDANT *on the children.*

MESSENGER.

Medea by Frederick Sandys

MEDEA

NURSE

WOULD the ship Argo ne'er had fetched her flight,
Twixt the dark Symplegades to Colchian land,
And the cleft pine in Pelion's woods ne'er fallen,
Nor caused the chieftains' hands to row, who went
To seek the golden fleece for Pelias,
For neither then Medea, mistress mine,
Had sailed to the Iolchian country's towers,
By love for Jason stricken at the heart;
Nor, having wrought upon the damsels, race
Of Pelias, to slay their sire, had dwelt
With husband and with sons in Corinth here,
So pleasuring in sooth the citizens
Of the country she has come to, by that flight,
Herself to Jason in all things conformed—
In which the better part of safety lies
That the woman should not differ from the man.
Now all's ajar and dearest love is sick:
For, his children and my mistress both betrayed,
Jason in royal spousals beds him, wed
To Creon's daughter, liege lord of this land.
But Medea, the forlorn, dishonoured cries
Upon his oaths, appeals to that chief troth
Of plighting hands, and calls the gods to mark
With what requital she from Jason meets.

Refusing food, her body anguish-prone,
Floating the hours from her in tears, she lies
Since first she knew her by her husband wronged;
And will not raise her eyes, nor from the ground
Lift up her face. As a rock might or sea-wave,
Does she hear those who love her counselling her,
Save when, averting her so pallid neck,
For her dear father she bemoans herself,
Her land and home deserted when she fled
With the man who does her this dishonour now.
She, hapless, sees now in her misery
What 'twere, not to have lost one's fatherland.
She loathes her sons, nor now joys seeing them.
Aye, but I dread her lest she plot some burst:
For she's high-stomached, nor will tamely bear
Wrongs put on her; I know her and I doubt her
Lest she slay those royal ones, yea and with them
The bridegroom, and go on to worser ills:
For she's unbending: not with ease, forsooth,
Will any sworn her foe chant victory.
But I perceive her boys, their races ceased,
Corning, unmindful of their mother's griefs;
For the young heart cares not to sorrow long.

ATTENDANT

Thou good old chattel of my lady's home,
Why, dawdling solitary at the gates,
Dost stand and croon of troubles to thyself?
Why has Medea willed thee leave her thus?

NURSE

Reverend attendant upon Jason's sons,
The masters' luck fallen wrong to worthy servants
Is their calamity and racks their hearts:
And I have reached to such a pitch of pain
That yearning came on me to pass out here
And cry to earth and heaven my lady's woes.

ATTENDANT

And she, sad woman, slacks not yet her moans?

NURSE

Hear him! Griefs at the start, not near half-way.

ATTENDANT

Oh fool—were't fit to speak thus of our lords—
How all unconscious of the newer ills!

NURSE

And what are they, old man? Grudge not to tell.

ATTENDANT

Nought. I am vexed for what's already said.

NURSE

By thy beard, hide nothing from thy fellow slave:
For I'll keep silence, if need be, on all.

ATTENDANT

I heard one say, I seeming not to hear,
As I came near the draught-boards where the old men
Around Pirene's sacred water sit,
That, with their mother, from the soil of Corinth,
The realm's lord, Creon, exiles presently
The boys. In sooth thus runs the tale: if true
I know not. But I pray it be not thus.

NURSE

What, and will Jason see his sons so used,
Even though he be in quarrel with their mother?

ATTENDANT

New ties stand foremost to the old. Henceforth
Towards this home he has no kindliness.

NURSE

We are undone then if to the first ill,
Ere yet it be drained dry, we add a new.

ATTENDANT

But thou, since for our lady to hear this
'Tis no fit time, peace and hush up the news.

NURSE

Oh children, hear ye what your father is?
I pray—no harm on him, he is my master;
But sure he is proved an ill friend to his kin.

ATTENDANT

What man is other? Dost thou learn but now
That each before his neighbour loves himself.
Some fairly, but some with the greed of gain?
As when, belike, for new espousals' sake
This father is no father to his sons.

NURSE

Go in the house boys: all will yet be well.
Thou, to the utmost, keep them by themselves,
Nor bring them near their sorrow-frenzied mother.
For late I saw her with the roused bull's glare
View them as though she'd at them. And I trow
That she'll not bate her wrath till it have swooped
On some prey. Be it foe then and not friend!

MEDEA (*heard speaking within*)

 Woe's me!
Forlorn that I am, borne down with despair!
Woe worth the while! If I might but die!

NURSE

There, 'tis as I said, your mother, dear boys,
Is lashing her will, is lashing her wrath:
Hurry on faster then into the house;
Approach ye not near her within her sight;
Go not to greet her; rather keep watch and ward
Against her wild mood and the virulent bent
 Of her ruthless mind.
Go, go, pass within, as you quickliest can.
It is plain to see that the cloud of grief,
Waxing and waxing since first it rose,
Will kindle ere long in stronger wrath.
And what will her passionate conquerless soul
 Stung by such wrongs compass then?

MEDEA (*still speaking within*)

 Ah me! ah me!
I have endured, sad woman, endured
A burden for great laments. Cursed sons
Of a loathed mother die, ye and your sire,
 And let all our house wane away!

NURSE

Woe worth the while! Sad woman, ah me!
But why are the boys made part in the crime
Of their father? Why turn on them? Alas,
Boys, how I anguish lest you come to harm.
Dread are the humours of princes: as wont
To be ruled in few things and in many to lord,
It is hard to them to turn from their wrath.
But to lead one's life in the level ways
Is best. Be it mine then to pass to old age
If no way high placed yet calmly secure.
For there's vantage just in speaking the name
Of the golden mean: and to have it and hold
Is past all best for man. But too high-pitched luck
Stands no mortal in stead at the time of need;
Nay, more, when the god is stirred to his wrath,
Dowers greater curse on the house.

CHORUS

I heard the voice, nay heard the shriek
   Of the hapless Colchian dame.
Is she not calmed? Old matron, speak—
   For through the double portals came
     A voice of wail and woe.
Nor, women, is it mine to share
Joy at this house's now despair,
   My friend from long ago.

NURSE

Here's no more a home, home-things are all fled;
For he is kept hence by a royal couch,
While in her chamber my lady alone
Weeps away life, and no way is calmed
    At heart by the words of her friends.

MEDEA (*still speaking within*)

    Woe! woe!
Oh lightning from heaven dart through my head!
For what is my gain to live any more?
Alas! alas! Might I cease in death,
    Escaping from hated life!

CHORUS

STROPHE

Oh Zeus dost thou perceive, and Earth, and Light,
What wail plains out the desolate young wife?
And why should love-pangs for thy wedded right,
Speed thee, poor fool, to end in death the strife?
    Nay, pray not so:
And if thine husband worship a new bride
Chafe not thyself—Zeus will judge on thy side—
Nor mourn thy spouse with too exceeding woe.

MEDEA (*still speaking within*)

Oh thou great Themis, and Sovereign Artemis,
Do you see what I bear, I who had bound
By terrible oaths my accursed spouse—
Whom with his bride may I one day behold
Crushed into atoms, they and their halls,
They who have dared the first wrong and on me?
Oh father! oh country! whom I forsook
Traitorous, slaying my brother first.

NURSE

Do ye hear how she speaks and makes her cry
To Themis invoked in the vow, and to Zeus,
Since he is deemed lord over mortal oaths?
It may not be that my lady shall stay
    Her rage with a little thing.

Chorus

ANTISTROPHE

Oh would she coming in our sight attend
That oracle of words we spake, if aught
May move her gloom and wrath. But never friend
Lack zeal of mine. Then go, let her be brought
    Hither outside the gate;
And bid her know me friend. But speed thee well,
Lest on those there with her some mischief fell
She wreak: so has her passion swelled of late.

NURSE

I will do as ye bid, but there's fear lest I fail
    My lady to win.
Yet I will give you my pains in free boon,
Although with the gaze of a lioness
With newborn cubs does she glare at her slaves,
If any approach her proffering speech.
And sure ye would not err if ye said
The men of old times were rude and nought wise,
Who fashioned for revels and wassails and feasts
Songs that make life by listening delight,
While no mortal has yet devised to lull
By music and chants many-toned the loathed pangs
When death and strange fates tread down homes.
And yet to calm these with the measured strain
Were in sooth a gain unto men: but why
Raise the vain sound where the feast is glad?
For the feast with its present fullness alone
    Is itself a delight for men.

CHORUS

    I heard a voice of sighs
    And groaning long laments,
    Where she, with shrilly cries,
    Her bitter anguish vents
Against the traitor her false lord,
And, bowed with wrong, she makes her prayer
To Themis, child of Zeus, whose care
    Is the plighted word—
    Themis, she
Who hither to our Hellas brought her,
Crossing o'er the night-dusk water,
The salt straits of the unending sea.

MEDEA

Women of Corinth, I come from the house
Lest ye should blame me. I know many men
Are counted arrogant, some that they keep from sight,
Some that they are in public, and to those
Who walk in calm comes ill repute of sloth.
For justice dwells not in the eyes of mortals,
Theirs who, before they inly know a man,
Look and straight loathe him, nothing wronged by him.
More, it behoves an alien specially
To mould himself unto the city's wont:
Nor can I praise a fractious citizen
Waxed wanton to his folk through ignorance.
But my soul by this all unlocked for weird
Fallen upon me is crushed utterly.
I am undone, and turned from joy of life,
My friends, I am in very need to die.
For he in whom was all to me, my husband,
Ye know it well, has proved of men most base.
Aye, of all living and of reasoning things
Are woman the most miserable race:
Who first needs buy a husband at great price,
To take him then for owner of our lives:
For this ill is more keen than common ills.
And of essays most perilous is this,
Whether one good or evil do we take.
For evil-famed to women is divorce,
Nor can one spurn a husband. She so brought
Beneath new rule and wont had surely need
To be a prophetess, unless at home
She learned the likeliest prospect with her spouse.
And if, we having aptly searched out this,
A husband house with us not savagely
Drawing in the yoke, ours is an envied life;

But if not, most to be desired is death.
And if a man grow sick to herd indoors,
He, going forth, stays his heart's weariness,
Turning him to some friend or natural peer;
But we perforce to one sole being look.
But, say they, we, while they fight with the spear,
Lead in our homes a life undangerous:
Judging amiss; for I would liefer thrice
Bear brunt of arms than once bring forth a child.
Ah well! the like words fit not thee and me:
For thee there is a country, and for thee
A father's home, for thee are life's delights
And the familiar intercourse of friends;
But I, alone, calling no city mine,
Am outraged by a spouse, I led a prey
From a far land, who have no mother more,
Nor brother, nor a kinsman of my blood,
Where to seek harbour in this evil day.
Therefore this much I fain would gain of you,
That, if I find a way and a device
To recompense my husband for these wrongs,
And her he wed and him who gave his daughter,
Ye will keep counsel. For in other things
Is a woman full of fears and most ill-fit
For battles and to look upon the sword;
But come there treason to her bridal bed
There is no other mind more thirsts for blood.

CHORUS

This will I do. For righteously wilt thou
Avenge thyself upon thy spouse, Medea:
Nor marvel I that thou dost mourn thy fate.
But I see Creon, sovereign of this land,
Approach, a messenger of new resolves.

CREON

Thee, sullen-browed and chafing at thy spouse,
Medea, I command that from this realm
Thou go an exile, taking thy two sons.
And linger not, for mine is the decree,
Nor will I enter in my house again
Till I have driven thee past this land's last bounds.

MEDEA

Alas! I hapless perish utterly!
For now my enemies crowd on all sail,
And there is no near haven from despair.
But yet, though bowed with wrongs, will I dare speak:
Why dost thou drive me from thy country, Creon?

CREON

I fear thee—it boots not to cloke my thoughts—
Lest thou shouldst work my child some mortal ill.
And many things make jointly to this dread.
Thou art much wise, and subtle in dread lores,
And thou art wroth, lorn of thy husband's bed;
Nay, I hear, threatst, so word came, some dire deed
On bridegroom and on bride and him who gave her.
Therefore I keep guard ere I surfer this.
Aye lady, better win thy present hate
Than, softened by thee, later mourn it long.

MEDEA

Ah me! Ah me!
Not now first, Creon, but a many times
Hath this fame stricken me and wrought me ill.
But never fits it one born prudent-souled
To have his children reared surpassing wise;
For, added to their blame of lavished time,
They win cross envy from their citizens.
For, offering a new wisdom unto fools,
Thou shalt be held a dullard not a sage:
And, if deemed more than those who make a show
Of varied subtleties, then shalt thou seem
A mischief in the city. Yea, myself
I share this fortune, for, being wise, I am
To some a mark for envy, and to some
Abhorrent. Yet I am not very wise.
But thou then fearest me lest thou feel some blow:
Things are not so with me—dread us not, Creon—
That I should do offence to kingly men.
For thou, how hast thou wronged me? Thou hast given
Thy girl what way thy mind led. But my husband
I hate. Yet thou, I think, in this didst well.
And now, in sooth, I grudge thee not thy luck:
Make marriages, be prosperous. But this land
Leave me, a home to dwell in: for, though wronged,
I will keep silence, vanquished by my lords.

CREON

Thou dost speak soft to hear; yet in my mind
Is fear lest thou be planning some foul deed,
And so much less I trust thee than before.
For a woman passionate, yea and a man,

Is easier warded than a silent plotter.
But go forth at the quickest, speak no word;
Since this is fixed, nor hast thou shift by which
Thou shalt stay with us, being my enemy.

MEDEA

Nay by thy knees, by thy new-wedded child!

CREON

Thou dost lose words. For thou shalt nought prevail.

MEDEA

But wilt thou exile me, nor heed my prayers?

CREON

Since thee I love not more than mine own house.

MEDEA

My country, how I now remember thee!

CREON

And next my children is my city dear.

MEDEA

Ah me! How great an ill to man is love!

CREON

That is, I doubt, as fortune waits on it.

MEDEA

Zeus, be it not hid from thee who caused these ills!

CREON

Hence, thou weak fool, and free me from these troubles.

MEDEA

I am the troubled, with full store of troubles.

CREON

Ere long my guards shall thrust thee out by force.

MEDEA

Nay, nay, not thus. Oh but I pray thee, Creon.

CREON

Thou wilt cause violence, woman, as I see.

MEDEA

We will go forth. I pleaded not of that.

CREON

Why dost thou strive then, nor wilt leave this realm?

MEDEA

Let me remain this one day and revolve
Some plan to fly, some refuge for my boys,
Since the father cares not for his sons to fend.
But pity them: thou also art a father,
And surely dost know natural tenderness.
For me, I care not if we must go forth,
But I weep them now schooled to adversity.

CREON

My mind by nature is nought tyrannous,
And oft by pity have I harmed myself:
And now I see, oh woman, that I err:
Yet shalt thou gain this. Yet I do forwarn thee,
If the next coming day's torch of the heavens
Shall see thee and thy boys in this realm's bounds,
Thou diest. The word that shall not swerve is spoken.

But now if stay thou must, stay this one day;
Not so thou'lt compass any deed I dread.

CHORUS

    Ah woman forlorn!
Alas for thee worn with thy miseries!
Where now wilt thou turn? with what sheltering host,
What country, what home, a haven for thee
    From woes wilt thou find?
Since the god, Medea, hath guided thy way
    Mid an issueless wave of woes.

MEDEA

On all sides woes are heaped: who shall deny it?
But it is not yet thus: believe it not.
Still waits there danger for the wedded pair,
And for the marriage-kinsfolk no light pangs.
For thinkest thou that ever I would thus
Have fawned on him wer't not to earn my vantage
And with a plot—no, not so much as spoken,
Not touched him with my hands. So he has reached
To such a folly that, when it was his
Driving me from his land to thwart my schemes,
He yields me that I stay here yet this day,
In which three of my foes I'll do to death,
The father, and the girl, and him my husband.
But, having many ways of death for them,
I know not, friends, which first to take in hand.
Whether shall I set fire to the bridal home,
Or, stealing silent to the nuptial bed,
Pash down my whetted dagger to the heart?

But there's one thing against me. Were I caught
Entering the house and working to mine ends,
Then would my death make laughter for my foes.
Better the easier way, and most akin
To my birthright skill, to take them off by drugs.
    So be it then.
They dead, what city shall receive me in?
What host will, offering me a land of refuge
And home assured, rescue my life? There's none.
Why then, still waiting for a little while
If any tower of safety show for us,
Silent and subtle I'll to this work of death.
But, if a fate resistless drives me forth,
Snatching the sword though 'twere to doom my death,
I'll slay them—yea to the very utmost dare.
For never, by my queen whom I revere
Beyond all else and chose unto my aid,
By Hecate who dwells on my hearth's shrine,
Shall any wring my heart and still be glad.
Aye, sad to them and bitter will I make
The wedding-tide, bitter the plighted bond
And my departing from this land. Go to,
Pondering and planning; spare no skill, Medea:
On to the deed, now is thy bravery tried.
Dost see thy hap? It fits not thou yield mirth
To the race of Sisyphus, Jason's new folk,
Thou born of a great sire, come of the Sun:
And thou art skilled. We women too art born
Most profitless indeed to noble works,
But cunningest devisers of all harms.

Chorus

STROPHE I

The hallowed rivers backward stream
Against their founts: right crooks awry
With all things else: man's every scheme
    Is treachery.
Even with gods faith finds no place.
But fame turns too: our life shall have renown:
Honour shall come to woman's race,
And envious fame no more weigh women down.

Chorus

ANTISTROPHE I

No more the staled songs shall be heard
Of muses hymning *our* deceit;
For Phœbus not on us conferred
    The lyre heaven-sweet
Lest we a counter strain should sing
Against the race of men: but ages old
Have in their keeping many a thing
Not of us only but of men to unfold.

Chorus

STROPHE II

And thou, grown mad at heart, didst come,
Sailed hither from thy father's home,
    Past the twin rocks of the sea,

And dwell'st upon an alien coast.
And now, sad woman, thou hast lost
The shelter that a wife's should be,
Thou widowed as thou art and sent
Dishonoured into banishment.

Chorus

ANTISTROPHE II

The sanctity of oaths is o'er:
Shame in great Hellas dwells no more,
    But is vanished into air.
Nor is there father's home for thee,
Forlorn one, where there yet might be
A harbour from thy storm of care:
And in thy house a dearer bride
Now queens it at thy husband's side.

JASON

Not the first time now, but often, have I seen
Fierce rage is an irremediable ill.
For thou, to whom remained this land and home,
Hadst thou borne meekly thy superiors' will,
Art by thy wild words driven from this realm.
And, for my part, no matter; never cease
From saying Jason is the worst of men:
But, for thy railing at the royal house,
Count it thy gain by exile to be punished.
For me I still was forward to appease
The princes' wrath, and would have had thee stay.
But thou, thou wouldest not leave thy folly, still

Railed at the royal house, and now indeed
Art driven from the realm. And yet I come,
Never weary for my friends, to care for thee,
That not in penury nor any want
Thou go forth with our children. Many hardships
Do wait on exile, and, though thou dost hate me,
I am not able to desire thy harm.

MEDEA

Oh wholly base this shall my tongue declare,
The greatest shame to thine unmanliness—
Thou comest to us, comest, our worst foe.
This is no courage, this no noble strength,
To front it out with friends whom thou hast wronged.
Rather it is man's loathsomest distemper,
Rank shamelessness. But thou dost well to come;
For I, reviling thee, will soothe my heart,
And thou wilt be stung hearing. Yea, and first
I from the first beginning will begin.
I saved thee, as each Hellene knows who sailed
In the ship Argo with thee, thee sent forth
To tame unto the yoke the fire-breathed bulls
And sow the furrow to the deadly strife:
And the dragon who, coiled round the golden fleece,
Fenced it with snaky knots and never slept,
I slew, who stood to thee thy beacon light:
And, traitress to my father and my home,
I, not so wise as loving, came with thee
To Peliot Iolchos: and by death
Of all kind bitterest, by his children's hands,
Pelias I slew and freed thee from all fear.
And, so much owing me, thou, oh worst villain,
Betrayest me and, father of my sons,

Hast a new wedding-bed. Sooth, hadst thou been
Yet childless thy desires had had excuse.
But the faith of oaths is gone, nor can I learn
If thou dost deem the gods no longer rule,
Or that new laws are now decreed for men,
Since thou dost own thyself perjured to me.
Alas this right hand thou didst often clasp!
These knees thou didst entreat by! To vain end
Was I polluted by this bad man's touch;
And all my hopes have ended in deceit.
Come now, I'll reason with thee as a friend—
Yet what way dreaming to get good of thee?
But still—for questioned thou wilt show more base—
Where shall I turn me? To my father's house
Which, with my country, I forsook for thee?
To Pelias' unhappy daughters? Sooth,
Kindly unto their house they'd welcome me
Who slew their father. For this is my case;
With my friends of home I have become at war,
And them whom it ill fitted me to wrong,
For thy sake I have made mine enemies.
And, truly, thou dost guerdon me with bliss
Envied by many a wife in Hellas, sure.
And truly a most perfect loyal spouse
Have I, poor wretch, if banished I go forth,
Barren of friends, alone with my lone children.
Rare fame for the new bridegroom that his sons
And she who saved him beggars roam about.
Oh Zeus why hast thou given mankind sure test
To know the spurious gold, while upon men
Is no mark born whereby to tell a knave?

CHORUS

Terrible is that anger, and to assuage
Most difficult, when friends with friends join battle.

JASON

It seems I'd needs be not unapt at words,
But like a skilful pilot sheer away,
Woman, from the jangling of thy wordy tongue.
But since thou dost so much exalt thy service,
I take it Cypris was, of gods and men,
Alone the guardian of my enterprise.
Why yes, thou hast a very crafty wit,
But 'twere invidious to go through the tale
How Eros, with his swift escapeless darts,
Forced it upon thee to preserve my life.
But not too nicely will I count our scores:
For how far thou didst help me 'twas not ill.
But in all truth thou hast for saving me
Gained far beyond thy giving: as I'll show.
First then, instead of thy barbarian land,
Thou dwellst in Hellas, and knowst justice now,
And the help of laws not measured by mere force:
And more, now all the Hellenes know thee wise,
And thou hast glory. But, hadst thou still dwelt
In those outmost shores, there were no word of thee.
And be it not mine to heap my house with gold,
Nor to sing sweeter strains than Orpheus,
If such my fortune make me not renowned.
So much then of thy troubles for my sake
I speak: since thou hast made this war of words.
But what thou twistst me with, my royal marriage,
In this I'll show thee, first that I was wise,

Then temperate, and to thee greatly kind
And to my boys. Nay, patience, hear me out
When I had come here from the Iolchian land,
Bringing with me a train of hindering cares,
What happier chance could I, an exile, find
Than this, to marry me with the king's child?
Not, thought which galls thee, sickened of thy bed
And wounded with desire for a new bride;
Nor striving for the crown of many sons—
For those I have suffice, I nought complain—
But, that which makes most, that we prosperous
Should dwell and not know scanting; well aware
That every friend will shun the poor man's path.
Also that I might rear as fits my house
My children, and, giving brothers to thy sons,
Bind them in one, and having interknit
My family, live on in happy case.
For what needst thou more children? But to me
'Tis profit to advance my living sons
By those that shall be. Have I ill resolved?
Thyself, wert thou not galled about thy bed,
Couldst never say it. But to such a pass
You women are come now, that, your bed safe,
You think you have everything; but let ill luck
Touch that, and all that fairest is and best
You count most hateful. 'Twere a goodly boon
If men could raise their children otherwhence
And there should be no woman tribe at all;
So would there be no mischief in the world.

CHORUS

Jason, these reasons hast thou tricked out well;
And yet, meseems, though I speak to thy distaste,
Thou dost not justly to betray thy wife.

MEDEA

Sure many ways from many men I differ.
For him who does wrong and is wise to gloze it
I hold worth worser doom. For making sure
He'll show wrong gracious with his tongue, he's bold
To every crime: yet he's not over wise—
As thou art not. Be no more specious with me
And cunning-phrased: one word o'ertopples thee;
It would have fitted thee, wert thou no knave,
To make this marriage with my won consent,
Instead of keeping secrecy from friends.

JASON

Rarely wouldst thou have humoured the design,
Had I shown thee the marriage, thou too weak
Even now to put away thy heart's mad rage.

MEDEA

This moved thee not. But with a foreign wife
Thou hadst gone unexalted to old age.

JASON

Now this well know: not for the woman's sake
I wed me in this royal home, now mine,
But, as I said but now, having at heart
To keep thee safe and to thy sons to add
Sons kingly born, a safeguard to our house.

MEDEA

Never be mine a lordly bitter life,
Nor wealth which makes me agony of soul.

JASON

Go to, reverse thy prayer and show more wise.
Never let fortune's goods seem bitter to thee,
Nor deem thyself unhappy while thou thrivst.

MEDEA

Yes, flout me, since thou hast a refuge thine:
But I shall desolate depart this land.

JASON

Thyself didst choose it: blame not any else.

MEDEA

By what deeds? Marrying and forsaking thee?

JASON

Cursing impious curses on the royal house.

MEDEA

And I through thy house verily am cursed.

JASON

Tush! I'll no more dispute with thee of this.
But if thou for thy children and thyself
Wouldst, as a help in flight, take of my goods,
Speak, I am prompt to give with no churl's hand,
And to pledged guest-friends who will use thee well
Send tokens of old hospitalities.
And, woman, dost thou nay-say these, thou'rt mad:
But ceasing from thy rage thou'lt softlier fare.

MEDEA

Guest-friends of thine shall never profit me.
Nor will I aught of thee: proffer me nothing,
For there's no service in a bad man's gift.

JASON

Then do I call the gods to witness this,
How I desire to serve thee and thy sons,
Yet thou'lt not like good gifts but wantonly
Dost spurn thy friends, therefore shalt mourn the more.

MEDEA

Begone, for longing after thy new bride
Seizes thee so much tarrying from her home:
Take her, for it is like—yea, and possessed
By a god I will declare it—thou dost wed
With such a wedding as thou'lt wish undone.

Chorus

STROPHE I

The wild loves that force eager way
Nor worth nor fame on man confer,
But if come Cypris with meet sway
There is no gracious god like her.
    Oh never, queen, I pray,
Drive from thy golden bow into my heart
The escapeless passion-poisoned dart.

Chorus

ANTISTROPHE I

But be my guardian chastity,
The god's best gift, nor let my mind,
By cruel Cypris forced awry,
The burden of hot anger find,
    Of gnawing jealousy;
But may she, pleasured with calm wedded lives,
Wisely adjudge their lots to wives.

STROPHE II

Oh home, oh country, ne'er may I
Through long hard years of poverty,
That bitterest of all distress,
Live on an alien citiless:
Nay, rather, having had my day,
Let death, let death do me away:
For no woe doth outpass this woe,
One's fatherland no more to know.

ANTISTROPHE II

Yes, we ourselves have seen, our speech
Is not of words that others teach,
Since, by most dread despair brought low,
Thee hath no city cared for, no,
Nor any friend. Let shameful blight
Slay him who gives not friends their right,
Unlocking them his heart's pure store:
Let him be friend of mine no more.

ÆGEUS

Medea, hail; since sooth no fairer greeting
Hath any known wherewith to reverence friends.

MEDEA

Oh hail, thou too, son of the wise Pandion,
Ægeus. Whence comst thou to this country's plains?

ÆGEUS

Last from the ancient oracle of Phœbus.

MEDEA

But wherefore sent to earth's prophetic centre?

ÆGEUS

Searching how children might be raised to me.

MEDEA

In heaven's name, leadst thou yet a childless life?

ÆGEUS

Childless am I by some divine one's will.

MEDEA

Hast thou a wife, or knowst no marriage-bed?

ÆGEUS

I am not unharnessed to the marriage yoke.

MEDEA

What then did Phœbus speak concerning sons?

ÆGEUS

Words subtler than a man can puzzle out.

MEDEA

Fits it I learn the sentence of the gods?

ÆGEUS

Surely—the more that it needs crafty wit.

MEDEA

What then declared he? Speak, if I may hear.

ÆGEUS

I might not loose the wine-bag's jutting foot.

MEDEA

Ere thou didst what or camst unto what land?

ÆGEUS

Ere to my father's hearth I came again.

MEDEA

Then seeking what to these shores didst thou sail?

ÆGEUS

There is one Pittheus who is king of Trœzen.

MEDEA

Of Pelops, so they say, most reverent son.

ÆGEUS

To him would I impart the god's reply.

MEDEA

For he is wise and in such matters versed.

ÆGEUS

And brother in arms to me most dear of all.

MEDEA

Now speed thee well, and gain what thou desirest.

ÆGEUS

But thou, why is thine eye dulled and thy bloom?

MEDEA

Ægeus, my husband is the chief of villains.

ÆGEUS

What sayest thou? Speak me plainly all thy cares.

MEDEA

Jason doth wrong me, nothing harmed by me.

ÆGEUS

By what deed done? Tell me more certainly.

MEDEA

Another wife is mistress of his home.

ÆGEUS

What! hath he ventured this most shameless thing?

MEDEA

Know it: I am dishonoured, I once dear.

ÆGEUS

Whether fallen amorous or hating thee?

MEDEA

Oh much enamoured! Faithless to old ties!

ÆGEUS

Why, let him go being, as thou sayst, a villain.

MEDEA

Of the king's alliance he fell amorous.

ÆGEUS

Who gives the bride then? Go through with the tale.

MEDEA

Creon, who governs this Corinthian realm.

ÆGEUS

Sooth, lady, if thou weepest there's excuse.

MEDEA

Undone! Aye, and from this land driven forth.

ÆGEUS

By whom? Thou dost show yet another ill.

MEDEA

Creon drives me from Corinthian ground an exile.

ÆGEUS

Will Jason suffer it? I praise not this.

MEDEA

Oh his words like it not; only he means
To bear it with a very valiant patience.
But thee, thee, I implore by this thy beard,
By these thy knees, and am thy suppliant,
Pity, pity me miserable wretch,
And never see me cast out desolate,
But take me to thy hearth in thy home and land.
So by the gods may thy desire of sons
Be brought to pass and mayst thou die content.
Aye, thou knowst not what find this thou hast found:
I'll stay thy childlessness, I'll have thee rear
A race of sons. Such philtres do I know.

ÆGEUS

For many reasons, lady, I am fain
This boon to give thee: for the gods' sake first:
Next for those sons whose birth thou dost assure;
For until now I am without all hope.
But 'tis thus with me: if indeed thou comst
Into my realm I will endeavour thee
Such host's protection as a just man may:
But this much, lady, I forewarn thee well,
I will not lead thee with me from this land;
Yet, if thyself thou comst into my house,
Thou shalt dwell sheltered and to none I'll yield thee.
Now from this soil thyself withdraw thy foot:
Both to my hosts and thee I would be leal.

MEDEA

It shall be thus. But, were an oath of this
Accorded me, all done by thee were gracious.

ÆGEUS

Dost thou not trust me? What disturbs thy faith?

MEDEA

I trust thee, but the house of Pelias
Now, is mine enemy, and Creon too.
Surely to these thou wouldst not, yoked by oaths,
Yield me if they would hale me from thy land:
But only bound by words, not sworn to the gods,
Thou mightest become their friend, mayhap be won
By herald-proffers: because I am weak,
But theirs are riches and a royal home.

ÆGEUS

Much foresight hast thou spoken, lady.   Now,
If it likes thee this should be, I gainsay not:
And unto me too were it the more safe
To have excuse to shew thine enemies,
And thou wert surer fenced. Name thou what gods.

MEDEA

Swear by the plains of Earth and by the Sun,
My father's father—add the gods' whole race.

ÆGEUS

To do what deed or what to do not? Speak.

MEDEA

Neither thyself ever to drive me forth
Out of thy land, nor, if some foe would take me,
To yield me in thy life of thy consent.

ÆGEUS

By Earth I swear, and the splendour of the Sun,
And all the gods, to stand by what thou sayst.

MEDEA

Enough. But, breaking faith, what curse on thee?

ÆGEUS

Such as do use to fall on impious men.

MEDEA

Depart in peace, for all is well: but I
With utmost speed will to thy realm repair,
Having ended that I do, gained that I long for.

CHORUS

Now Maia's son, the wayfarer's lord,
   Bring thee to thy home:
And that next thy heart, which thou eagerest for,
Mayst thou attain; for a noble man,
   Ægeus, thou seemst unto me.

MEDEA

Oh Zeus, and Right the child of Zeus, and thou
Light of the Sun! Now, now, friends, shall be mine
A goodly victory on mine enemies,
And I do tread the path: now is there hope
Mine enemies shall pay the penalty.
For this man, when I was in greatest stress,
Reveals himself a harbour for my schemes:
To whom my mooring tackle will I fix,
Having reached the town and citadel of Pallas.
And now to thee I'll speak all my resolves:
Hearken then words tuned to no pleasant mirth.
Sending one of my household I'll intreat
That Jason come into my sight: he come,
I'll speak him meek sweet words—as that his doings
Seem goodly to me and become him well;
Then I'll implore him that my sons may stay—
Not in an unkind land to leave my children

To the despitings of mine enemies,
But to destroy the king's child by my wiles:
For I will send them, holding gifts in hand,
To bear the bride, that they be not driven hence,
And if she take the gauds and prank her in them
She shall die horribly, and with her too
Whoso shall touch the girl: with such rare salves
Will I anoint the gifts. Thus then I end
That theme. But I am woe for what a deed
Needs must be done: for I shall slay my sons.
No one there is who may deliver them.
And, having hurled down the whole house of Jason,
I shall go forth this land, flying the curse
Of my dear children's death and having borne
To do the most unhallowed of all deeds.
For, oh my friends, the mockeries of foes
May not be borne. Well, be it as it must be.
What good for me to live? No home for me,
Nor fatherland, nor refuge from my woes.
Oh then I erred when I went forth and left
My father's house lured by a Hellene's talk,
Who, with the god's help, shall pay forfeit yet.
For neither shall he more behold alive
His sons by me nor shall his new made wife
Bear to him other sons, since the ill wench
Shall die an ill death, doomed by my drugged salves.
Let none believe me weak and lethargic
Nor tame in spirit, but far other souled;
Dour to my foes, but to my friends most helpful:
For the lives of such do wear the nobler grace.

CHORUS

Now, since thou hast possessed us of thy thought,
Much anxious both to serve thee and give help
To human laws, I urge thee, do not thus.

MEDEA

It may no otherwise. But 'tis excused
That thou so speak'st, who bear'st not wrongs as I.

CHORUS

But, lady, hast thou heart to kill thy sons?

MEDEA

Since thus my husband's heart were deepest stung.

CHORUS

But thou wert then the woefullest of women.

MEDEA

So be it. Wasted are all tempering words.
              (*To the Nurse*)
But thou, go, speed thee and bring Jason here;
For I do use thee in all trusty things.
But nothing speak of that I have resolved
If thou mean thy mistress well and be true woman.

Chorus

STROPHE I

The Athenians, great from long ago,
And children of the gods in heaven,
Still for their daily nurture know
The loftiest food of wisdom given
A hallowed and unconquered state;
And, through their bright translucent air,
Move ever with proud jubilant gait,
    There, as old rhymes relate,
Where erst Harmonia, of the yellow hair,
The virgin nine Pierian muses bare.

ANTISTROPHE I

There too, the ancient lay runs thus,
Once Cypris, quaffing from the wave
Of crystal flowing Cephissus,
O'er all the land her soft breath drave
In tender wafts of scented wind:
And, donning ever her sweet crown
Of rose-bloom in her loose locks twined,

Her vassal loves, assigned
Kind ministers to wisdom, she sends down,
And helpmates in all deeds of good renown.

　　　　　　　STROPHE II

　　　The land of sacred waters, then,
　　　The city of good will to men,
　　　How shall it have a welcoming
　　　For thee, a too unholy thing
　　　To dwell with others, murderess thou
　　　Of thine own children? Oh, take heed;
　　　Think, think on thy sons' death-blow now;
　　　Think, think upon thy deadly deed.
　　　Nay, by thy knees, by every prayer,
　　　We all invoke thee, oh forbear:
　　　Thou shalt not slay thy sons: forbear.

　　　　　　　ANTISTROPHE II

　　　And how then couldst thou ever find
　　　Force in thy hand, thy heart, thy mind,
　　　Against thy sons, thine own, to wreak
　　　The dreadful vengeance thou dost seek?
　　　And how, if but a moment long
　　　Upon thy sons thy glance should wait,
　　　Wilt thou indeed continue strong
　　　And tearless to fulfil their fate?
　　　It is not thine, not possibly,
　　　When at thy feet the children cry
　　　In their life-blood thy fell hand to dye.

JASON

Summoned, I come. For, though thou'rt rancourous,
Thou shalt not fail of this, but I will hear,
Lady, what new boon thou wouldst have of me.

MEDEA

Jason, I pray thee, be to my past words
Forgiving. For thou shouldst bear with my passion,
Since once there was much love between us two.
But I have taken counsel with myself
And chid me: "Oh cross fool, why do I rave,
And am in wrath at those who plan me good?
And why stand I at war with this realm's lords
And with my husband who, in that he does,
Does it for our most profit, marrying him
A royal bride and giving my sons brothers?
Shall I not turn from anger? What my hurt,
For whom the gods so graciously provide?
Truly have I not children, and do know
We are but fugitives and poor of friends?"
And, having pondered these things, I discerned
My much unreason and how fond my rage.
Now therefore I approve, and politic
Account thee taking to us this alliance,
But myself witless, I who should have shared
Thy counsels with thee and accomplished them,
Stood by the bed and joyed to tend the bride.
But what we are we are—I'll say no worse—
Women. Then fits not thou shouldst even thee
To baseness nor with folly answer folly.
I do submit and say I then judged ill,
But now I wiselier have resolved of this.

Boys, boys, come hither, quit the house, approach,
Greet ye your father, speak to him with me,
And from the former hatred be now changed,
Together with your mother, into friends.
For we've made covenant, and laid by wrath.
Take his right hand—Ah me! the woeful day!—
Lo what unshaped forebodings vex my soul!
Why, children, ye will thus, in a long life
Stretch forth your dear arms to him? Oh poor me,
How prone to weep am I and full of dread.
But, freeing me of quarrel with your father,
My trembling sight has filled itself with tears.

CHORUS

In mine eyes too the dewy tear hath sprung—
And may the present ill not pass to worse.

JASON

Lady, these words I praise, nor blame the former;
For 'tis of woman's kind against a spouse
Trafficking in new marriages to rage.
Now to the better part thine heart has turned,
And thou, though late, dost own the mastering will.
Conduct of a wise woman, this. For you,
My boys, your father, not uncarefully,
Has spent much forethought with the gods' good help,
Since you, I trow, shall with your brothers yet
Be first in Corinth's land. But grow and thrive:
The rest your father or what god is kind
Will bring about. And may I see you bloom
Waxed to youth's prime, triumphant on my foes.

Thou why with new tears dost thou dew thine eyes,
Turning thy wan cheek from me, nor dost greet
With any gladness yet these words of mine?

MEDEA

'Tis nothing. I am troubled for my sons.

JASON

Be of good courage: I will care for them.

MEDEA

I will. Surely I shall not doubt thy word.
But woman's a poor she thing and born to cry.

JASON

Why, prithee, for the boys make such laments?

MEDEA

I gave them birth: and when thou didst speak hopes
The boys should live, a qualm came over me
Whether it should go thus. Well, but why now
Thou hast this talk with me is told in part;
Of the rest I will make mention. Since it hath pleased
The royal house to send me from the land,
For me too it is best, I know it well,

Not to dwell here, a thwarting thing to thee
And to the country's sovereigns. For I seem
As though I had a quarrel to their house.
But verily we'll hasten from this land.
And yet, that thine own hand may train the boys,
Pray Creon that they shall not leave his realm.

JASON

It must be tried. With what success I know not.

MEDEA

Why then, bid thou thy wife entreat her father
To the end the children shall not leave his realm.

JASON

Certes. I look too to prevail with her,
If she be such as other women are.

MEDEA

I too will share with thee in the attempt,
For I will send her gifts more beautiful
By far than are among men now, I know:
A fine-webbed robe and garland of wrought gold:
My sons shall bear them. Now then with all haste
Let some one of my servants bring the gauds.
She shall be rich, not in one thing but many,
Gaining thee a perfect husband to her spouse,

And having hers the gauds which erst the Sun,
My father's father, gave those born from him.
Boys, take this wedding dower into your hands,
Carry them to the happy royal bride:
Give them—she will not have unworthy gifts.

JASON

Yet why, fond fool, lose these out of thy keep?
Dost think the kingly house is scant of robes?
Or gold, dost think? Preserve these, give them not:
For, if my wife set any store on me,
I well know she will prize me over bribes.

MEDEA

Thwart me not. Gifts, they say, win even gods,
And gold makes more with men than countless reasons.
Fate sides with her; the god exalts her now;
She queens it young. But I, not with mere gold,
With my own life, would buy my sons from exile.
Come, children, go now to her lordly home,
Go to your father's new wife and my mistress,
Pray her, beseech, that ye leave not this realm,
Offering the gauds: for chiefly it behoves
That she receive our gifts in her own hands.
Go with all haste. And may you to your mother
Become glad messengers of that she hopes.

Chorus

STROPHE I

No hope left us now for the children's life;
No hope; they are passing on to death;
And the gift that comes to the new-made wife
Is the gift of a curse in her golden wreath.
    Alas for her doom!
Round about her yellow hair
Her own hand will set it there,
Signet jewel of the tomb.

ANTISTROPHE I

By the grace and the perfect gleaming won
She will place the gold-wrought crown on her head,
She will robe herself in the robe; and anon
She will deck her a bride among the dead.
    Alas for her doom!
  Fallen in such snare, too late
  Would she struggle from her fate,
Hers the death-lot of the tomb.

STROPHE II

But thou, oh wretched man, oh woeful-wed,
Yet marriage-linked to kings; thou all unseeing,
    Who nearest fast
A swift destruction to thy children's being,
A hateful death to her who shares thy bed,
Oh hapless man, how fallen from thy past!

ANTISTROPHE II

And miserable mother of fair boys,
We mourn too thy despair with outburst weeping,
    Thine who wouldst kill
Thy sons for the wife's couch where lonely sleeping
Thy husband leaves thee for new lawless joys
With a new homemate who thy place shall fill.

ATTENDANT

Mistress, thy children are forgiven from exile:
And in her hands the queenly bride, well pleased,
Received the gifts. Thence goodwill to thy sons.

MEDEA

Alas!

ATTENDANT

Why dost thou stand aghast when thou hast prospered?

MEDEA

Woe's me!

ATTENDANT

This chimes not with the tidings I declare.

MEDEA

Woe's me again.

ATTENDANT

I have not heralded mischance I know not,
And missed my joy of bringing happy news?

MEDEA

Thou hast brought what thou hast brought: I blame thee not.

ATTENDANT

Why then dost droop thine eyes and dost weep tears?

MEDEA

There is much cause, old man. For this the gods
And I by my own wild resolves have wrought.

ATTENDANT

Take heart. For through thy sons thou'lt yet return.

MEDEA

Alas, I shall send others home ere that.

ATTENDANT

Thou'rt not the only one torn from her sons,
And being mortal lightly shouldst bear griefs.

MEDEA

And so I will. But go thou in the house,
Prepare my children what the day requires.
Oh sons, my sons, for you there is a home
And city where, forsaking wretched me,
Ye shall still dwell and have no mother more:
But I, an exile, seek another land,
Ere I have joyed in you and seen you glad,
Ere I have decked for you the nuptial pomp,
The bride, the bed, and held the torch aloft.
Oh me! forlorn by my untempered moods!
In vain then have I nurtured ye, my sons,
In vain have toiled and been worn down by cares,
And felt the hard child-bearing agonies.
There was a time when I, unhappy one,
Had many hopes in you, that both of you
Would cherish me in age and that your hands,
When I am dead, would fitly lay me out—
That wish of all men: but now lost indeed
Is that sweet thought, for I must, reft of you,
Live on a piteous life and full of pain:
And ye, your dear eyes will no more behold
Your mother, gone into your new strange life.
Alas! Why do ye fix your eyes on me,
My sons? Why smile ye on me that last smile?
Alas! What must I do? For my heart faints,
Thus looking on my children's happy eyes.
Women, I cannot. Farewell my past resolves.

My boys go forth with me. What boots it me
To wring their father with their cruel fates,
And earn myself a doubled misery?
It shall not be, shall not. Farewell resolves.
And yet what mood is this? Am I content
To spare my foes and be a laughing-stock?
It must be dared. Why, out upon my weakness
To let such coward thoughts steal from my heart!
Go, children, to the house. And he who lacks
Right now to stand by sacrifice of mine,
Let him look to it. I'll not stay my hand.
     Alas! alas!
No surely. Oh my heart thou canst not do it;
Racked heart, let them go safely, spare the boys:
Living far hence with me they'll make thee joy.
No; by the avenging demon-gods in hell,
Never shall be that I should yield my boys
To the despitings of mine enemies.
For all ways they must die, and, since 'tis so,
Better I slay them, I who gave them birth.
All ways 'tis fated: there is no escape.
For now, in the robes, the wealth upon her head,
The royal bride is perishing; I know it.
But, since I go on so forlorn a journey
And them too send on one yet more forlorn,
I'd fain speak with my sons. Give me, my children,
Give your mother your right hands to clasp to her.
Oh darling hands, oh dearest lips to me,
Oh forms and noble faces of my boys!
Be happy: but *there*. For of all part here
Your father has bereft you. Oh sweet kiss,
Oh grateful breath and soft skin of my boys!
Go, go. I can no longer look on you,
But by my sufferings am overborne.
Oh I do know what sorrows I shall make,

But anger keeps the mastery of my thoughts,
Which is the chiefest cause of human woes.

CHORUS

Oftentimes now have I ere to-day
Reached subtler reasons, joined higher debates,
Than womanhood has the right to scan.
But 'tis that with us too there walks a muse
Discoursing high things yet not to us all,
Since few of the race of women there be,
(Thou wert like to find among many but one),
    Not friendless of any muse.
And now I aver that of mortals those
Who have never wed, or known children theirs,
    Than parents are happier far.
For the childless at least, through not making essay
If sons be born for a joy or a curse,
Having none are safe from much miseries.
But such as have springing up in their homes
Sweet blossom and growth of children, them
I see worn with cares through the weary while:
First how to rear them in seemly wise
And how to leave the children estate;
Then next, whether they are spending themselves
For ignoble beings or for good,
    That is left dark from their ken.
But one last ill of all to all men
Now will I speak. For if they have found
Sufficing estate, and their children have waxed
To the glory of youth, and moreover are good,
If their lot have chanced to them thus, lo Death,
Vanished back to his Hades again,
Has snatched the forms of the children away.

And what avails it for children's sake
To have the gods heap on mortals' heads
    This bitterest deadly despair?

MEDEA

Friends, now for long abiding the event,
Eager I gaze for what shall come of it;
And now discern a servitor of Jason's
Advancing hither. And his gasping breath
Declares him messenger of some dire news.

MESSENGER

Oh thou who hast wrought a horrible wild deed,
Medea, fly, fly, sparing not car of the waves
Nor chariot hurrying thee across the plains.

MEDEA

But what hath chanced to me worth such a flight?

MESSENGER

The royal maiden is this moment dead,
With Creon her father, by thy magic drugs.

MEDEA

Thou hast told sweetest news. From henceforth rank
Among my benefactors and my friends.

MESSENGER

What sayst thou? Lady, hast thou thy right wits,
Nor ravst, who, having outraged the king's hearth,
Joyst at the hearing and dost nothing fear?

MEDEA

Somewhat in sooth I have to answer back
To these thy words. But be not hasty, friend.
Come, tell me how they died. For twice so much
Wilt thou delight me if they died in torments.

MESSENGER

When then the boys, thy two sons, had arrived,
And with their father entered the bride's house,
We servants, who were troubled for thy griefs,
Rejoiced: and much talk shortly filled our ears,
Thou and thy husband had made up past strife.
One kissed the hand and one the golden head
Of thy young sons, and I myself, for joy,
Followed the boys into the women's halls.
But our mistress, whom we serve now in thy place,
Before she saw thy sons come side by side
Kept her glad gaze on Jason: then ere long
She hid her eyes and turned away from him

Her whitened face, loathing the boys' approach.
But thy husband checked his young bride's heat and rage,
Thus speaking, "Be not rancorous to thy friends,
But cease thy wrath and turn again thy head,
Counting those dear who're to thy husband dear.
Take then their gifts, and of thy father pray
He spare for my sake my boys' banishment."
And when she saw the gauds she said no nay,
But spoke her husband sooth in all. And ere
The father and the boys had gone far forth
She took the shimmering robes and put them on,
And, setting round her curls the golden crown,
At the bright mirror stroked her tresses right,
And smiled on the mute likeness of herself.
Next, risen from her couch, flits through the room,
Daintily tripping on her milk-white feet,
With the gifts overjoyed, often and long
O'er her slant shoulder gazing on herself.
But then a sight came dread to look upon;
For, a change come on her hue, she staggers back,
Shuddering in every limb, and scarce wins time
To fall upon her couch, not to the ground.
Then an old waiting dame, who deemed the wrath
Of Pan or other god had come on her,
Shrilled the prayer-chaunt; I trow before she saw
The white foam oozing through the mouth, the eyes
Start from their sockets strained, the bloodless flesh.
For then, far other wailing than her chaunt,
Came her great shriek. Straight, to the father's house
Rushed one, another to the new-wed husband,
To tell of the bride's fate; and all the house
Was ringing with incessant hurrying steps.
By this might a swift walker stretching limb
Have touched the goal of the six plethra course,
And she, who had been speechless, with shut eyes,

Fearfully moaned, poor wretch, and started up:
For twofold anguish did make war on her.
For both the golden crown set round her head
Was sending marvellous streams of eating fire,
And the fine-webbed robe, the offering of thy sons,
Was gnawing at the hapless one's white flesh.
But she, sprung from her couch, now flies, ablaze,
Tossing her head and curls this way and that,
Fain to dash off the crown. But all too firm
The golden headband clave; and still the fire
Flamed doubly fiercer when she tossed her locks,
And, conquered by her fate, she drops to the floor;
Scarce, but by her own father to be known:
For neither the grave sweetness of her eyes
Nor her fair face was visible; but blood
Mingled with flame was welling from her head,
And, by the secret poison gnawed, her flesh
Dropped from the bones, as resin-gouts from the fir—
Dreadful to see. And none dared touch the dead.
For her fate had we to our monitor.
But the hapless father, through his ignorance
Of how she perished, having ere we knew
Entered the chamber, falls upon the corse,
Breaks instant into wailing, and, her body
Enfolded in his clasp, he kisses her
Thus calling on her, "Oh unhappy child,
What god hath foully done thee thus to death?
Who makes this charnel heap of mouldering age
Thy childless mourner? Oh woe worth the while!
Would now that I might die with thee, my child."
But, when he stayed his sobbings and laments
And would have raised his aged body up,
He, as the ivy by the laurel's boughs,
By the fine-webbed robes was caught; and fearful grew
The struggle. He sought on his knees to rise:

She held him back. And if by force he rose
He tore the aged flesh from off his bones.
And then at length the evil-fated man
Ceased and gave up the ghost, able no more
To cope with that great anguish. And they lie,
Father and daughter, corpses side by side:
A sight of sorrow that appeals for tears.
And truly let thy fortunes be apart
From reasonings of mine: for thou thyself
Wilt know a shelter from the retribution.
But not now first I count the lot of man
A passing shadow: and I might say those
Of mortals who are very seeming wise
And fret themselves with learnings, those are they
Who make them guilty of the chiefest folly;
But no one mortal is a happy man,
Though, riches flooding in, more prosperous
One than another grow; yet none is happy.

CHORUS

Fortune, it seems, on Jason will to-day
Justly heap many woes. Oh hapless one,
Daughter of Creon, how we mourn thy fate,
Who to the halls of Hades art gone forth
Because of Jason's marrying with thee.

MEDEA

My friends, this purpose stand approved to me,
Slaying my boys to hurry from this realm;
Not, making weak delays, to give my sons
By other and more cruel hands to die.

Nay, steel thyself my heart. Why linger we
As not to do that horror which yet must be?
Come, oh my woeful hand, take take the sword:
On to my new life's mournful starting point,
And be no coward, nor think on thy boys,
How dear, how thou didst give them birth. Nay rather
For this short day forget they are thy sons:
Then weep them afterwards. For though thou slay'st them
Oh but they're dear, and I a desolate woman.

Chorus

strophe

Earth, and all-lighting glow of Sun,
    Behold, behold;
See this sad woman and undone,
Ere yet her murderous hand, made bold
Against her own, her children slay.
For they sprang of the golden stem
Of thy descent; and great to-day
Our dread the blood of gods in them
Shall by a mortal's wrath be spilt.
But now do thou, oh Zeus-born light,
Stay her, prevent; put thou to flight
That fell Erinnys to this home
From gods avenging past crimes come
To whelm her in despair and guilt.

ANTISTROPHE

Upon thy children has thy care
    Been spent in vain;
In vain thy loved babes didst thou bear;
Thou who the inhospitable lane
Of the dark rocks Symplegades
Didst leave behind thee in thy wake.
Forlorn one, why do pangs like these
Of passion thy torn spirit shake?
Why shall stern murder of them grow?
For scarce is any cleansing found
Of kindred blood that from the ground
For vengeance cries: but like for like
The gods send curses down and strike
The slayers and their houses low.

FIRST SON

Alas!
What shall I do? Whither run from our mother?

SECOND SON

I know not, dearest brother, for we perish.

CHORUS

Dost hear thy children, hear their cry of pain?
    Oh luckless woman, desperate!
Shall I within the house then? I were fain
    To shield the children from such fate.

FIRST SON

Ho! in the gods' name, rescue! There is need.

SECOND SON

For we are in the toils, beneath the knife.

CHORUS

Oh cruel, what, of stone or steel art thou,
    Thou who that bloom
Of sons thyself didst bear wouldst see die now
    By thine hands' doom?
One woman have I heard of, one alone
And of the far-off days, whose deathful hand
Was laid upon the babes that were her own,
Ino by gods distraught when from her land
She by the queenly spouse of Zeus was banned,
    Sent to roam to and fro;
And, seeking her sons' death, she, wild with woe,
Stretched forth her foot from off the sea's rough strand,
Whelmed her with them into the waves below,
    And, they so dying with her, died.
Henceforth can aught called strange or dread betide?
Oh bed of woman, with all mischief fraught,
What ills hast thou ere now to mortals brought!

JASON

Women, ye who thus stand about the house,
Is she within her home who wrought these crimes,
Medea, or hath she gone away in flight?
For now must she or hide beneath the earth
Or lift herself with wings into wide air
Not to pay forfeit to the royal house.
Thinks she, having slain the rulers of this land,
Herself uninjured from this home to fly?
But not of her I reck as of my sons:
Her those she wronged will evilly requite,
But to preserve my children's life I came,
Lest to my hurt the avenging kin on them
Wreak somewhat for their mother's bloody crime.

CHORUS

Oh wretched man! What woes thou comst to, Jason,
Thou knowst not, else hadst thou not said these words.

JASON

What is it? Seeks she then to kill me too?

CHORUS

The boys have perished by their mother's hand.

JASON

Woe! What sayst thou? Woman, how thou destroyst me!

CHORUS

As now no more in being count thy sons.

JASON

Where killed she them, in the house or without?

CHORUS

Open these gates, thou'lt see thy murdered sons.

JASON

Undo the bolt on the instant, servants there,
Loose the clamps, that I may see my grief and bane,
May see them dead and guerdon her with death.

MEDEA (*from overhead*)

Why dost thou batter at these gates, and force them,
Seeking the dead and me who wrought their deaths?
Cease from this toil. If thou hast need of me
Speak then, if thou wouldst aught. But never more
Thy hand shall touch me; such a chariot
The Sun, my father's father, gives to me,
A stronghold from the hand of enemies.

JASON

Oh loathsome thing, oh woman most abhorred
Of gods and me and all the race of men,
Thou who hast dared to thrust the sword in thy sons
Thyself didst bear, and hast destroyed me out,
Childless. And thou beholdest sun and earth,
Who didst this, daredst this most accursed deed!
Perish. Oh, I am wise now, then unwise,
When from thy home in thy barbarian land
I brought thee with me to a Hellene house,
A monstrous bane; to the land that nurtured thee
And to thy father traitress. Now at me
Have the gods launched thy retributory fiends,
Who, slaying first thy brother at the hearth,
Hiedst thee unto the stately-prowed ship Argo.
Such thy first deeds: then, married to myself
And having borne me children, for a spite
Of beddings and weddings thou hast slaughtered them.
There's not a Hellene woman had so dared;
Above whom I, forsooth, choose thee to wife—
A now loathed tie and ruinous to me—
Thee lioness not woman, of a mood
Than the Tursenian Scylla more untamed.
Enough; for not with thousands of rebukes
Could I wring thee, such is thine hardihood.
Avaunt, thou guilty shame! child-murderess!
But mine it is to wail my present fate;
Who nor of my new spousals shall have gain,
Nor shall have sons whom I begot and bred,
To call my living own: for I have lost them.

MEDEA

I would have largely answered back thy words
If Zeus the father knew not what from me
Thou didst receive and in what kind hast done.
And 'twas not for thee, having spurned my love,
To lead a merry life, flouting at me,
Nor for the princess; neither was it his
Who gave her thee to wed, Creon, unscathed,
To cast me out of this his realm. And now,
If it is so like thee, call me lioness
And Scylla, dweller on Tursenian plains,
For as right bade me I have clutched thy heart.

JASON

And thou too sufferest, partner in the pangs.

MEDEA

True, but the pain profits if thou shalt not flout.

JASON

Oh sons, how foul a mother have ye had!

MEDEA

Oh boys, how died ye by your father's guilt!

JASON

Not this right hand of mine slew them, indeed.

MEDEA

No, but thine outrage and new wedding ties.

JASON

So for a bed lost thou thoughtst fit to slay them?

MEDEA

Dost thou count that a light wrong to a woman?

JASON

Aye, to a chaste one: but thou'rt wholly base.

MEDEA

They are no more. For this will torture thee.

JASON

They are, I say—a haunting curse for thee.

MEDEA

Who first begun the wrong the gods do know.

JASON

Thy loathly mind they verily do know.

MEDEA

Thou'rt hateful: and I'm sick of thy cross talk.

JASON

And I of thine: but the farewell is easy.

MEDEA

Well, how? What shall I do? I too long for it.

JASON

Let me then bury and bemoan these dead.

MEDEA

Never. Since I will bury them with this hand,
Bearing them to the sacred grove of Hera,
God of the heights, that no one of my foes
Shall do despite to them, breaking their graves.
And I'll appoint this land of Sisyphus
A solemn high day and a sacrifice
For aye, because of their unhallowed deaths.
But I go to the city of Erechtheus,
To dwell with Ægeus there, Pandion's son.
For thee, as is most fit, thou, an ill man,
Shalt die an ill death, thy head battered in
By the ruins of thine Argo: that, to thee,
The sharp last sequel of our wedding tie.

JASON

But thee may thy children's Erinnys slay
    And Vengeance for blood.

MEDEA

And who among gods and friends will hear thee,
Betrayer of strangers and breaker of oaths?

JASON

Out, out, stained wretch and child murderess.

MEDEA

Go now to thy home and bury thy bride.

JASON

I go. Yea, of both my children bereft.

MEDEA

Thy wail is yet nothing. Wait and grow old.

JASON

Oh, sons, much loved!

MEDEA

    Of their mother not thee.

JASON

And yet thou didst slay them.

MEDEA

        Making thee woe.

JASON

Alas! alas! I, a woeful man,
Desire to kiss the dear lips of my boys.

MEDEA

Thou callst on them now, hast welcomes now;
Then didst reject them.

JASON

In the gods' name,
Give me to touch my children's soft flesh.

MEDEA

It may not be: thy words are vain waste.

JASON

Oh Zeus, dost thou hear how I'm kept at bay,
And this that is done unto me of her,
This foul and child-slaying lioness?
But still to my utmost as best I may
I make these death-wails and invokings for them;
Thus to my witness calling the gods,
How them, having slain my sons, dost prevent
That I touch with my hand and bury the dead—
Whom would I had never begotten so
By thee to behold them destroyed.

CHORUS

Zeus in Olympus parts out many lots,
And the gods work to many undreamed of ends,
And that we looked for is never fulfilled,
And to things not looked for the gods make a way:
    Even so hath this issue been.

MEDEA IN ATHENS

Augusta Webster,
Portraits, 1870

Dead is he? Yes, our stranger guest said dead—
said it by noonday, when it seemed a thing
most natural and so indifferent
as if the tale ran that a while ago
there died a man I talked with a chance hour
when he by chance was near me. If I spoke
"Good news for us but ill news for the dead
when the gods sweep a villain down to them,"
'twas the prompt trick of words, like a pat phrase
from some one other's song, found on the lips
and used because 'tis there: for through all day
the news seemed neither good nor ill to me.

And now, when day with all its useless talk
and useless smiles and idiots' prying eyes
that impotently peer into one's life,
when day with all its seemly lying shows
has gone its way and left pleased fools to sleep,
while weary mummers, taking off the mask,
discern that face themselves forgot anon
and, sitting in the lap of sheltering night,
learn their own secrets from her—even now
does it seem either good or ill to me?
No, but mere strange.

                And this most strange of all
that I care nothing.

                  Nay, how wild thought grows.
Meseems one came and told of Jason's death:
but 'twas a dream. Else should I, wondering thus,
reck not of him, nor with the virulent hate
that should be mine against mine enemy,
nor with that weakness which sometimes I feared
should this day make me, not remembering Glaucè,
envy him to death as though he had died mine?

  Can he be dead? It were so strange a world
with him not in it.

           Dimly I recall
some prophecy a god breathed by my mouth.
It could not err. What was it? For I think;—
it told his death.

              Has a god come to me?
Is it thou, my Hecate? How know I all?
For I know all as if from long ago:
and I know all beholding instantly.
Is not that he, arisen through the mists?—
a lean and haggard man, rough round the eyes,
dull and with no scorn left upon his lip,
decayed out of his goodliness and strength;
a wanned and broken image of a god;
dim counterfeit of Jason, heavily
wearing the name of him and memories.

And lo, he rests with lax and careless limbs
on the loose sandbed wind-heaped round his ship
that rots in sloth like him, and props his head

on a half-buried fallen spar. The sea,
climbing the beach towards him, seethes and frets,
and on the verge two sunned and shadowed clouds
take shapes of notched rock-islands; and his thoughts
drift languid to the steep Symplegades
and the sound of waters crashing at their base.

And now he speaks out to his loneliness
"I was afraid and careful, but she laughed:
'Love steers' she said: and when the rocks were far,
grey twinkling spots in distance, suddenly
her face grew white, and, looking back to them,
she said, 'Oh love, a god has whispered me
'twere well had we died there, for strange mad woes
are waiting for us in your Greece': and then
she tossed her head back, while
her brown hair streamed
gold in the wind and sun, and her face glowed
with daring beauty, 'What of woes', she cried,
'if only they leave time for love enough?'
But what a fire and flush! It took one's breath!"
And then he lay half musing, half adoze,
shadows of me went misty through his sight.

   And bye and bye he roused and cried "Oh dolt!
Glaucè was never half so beautiful."
Then under part-closed lids remembering her,
"Poor Glaucè, a sweet face, and yet methinks
she might have wearied me:" and suddenly,
smiting the sand awhirl with his angry hand,
scorned at himself "What god befooled my wits
to dream my fancy for her yellow curls
and milk-white softness subtle policy?
Wealth and a royal bride: but what beyond?
Medea, with her skills, her presciences,

man's wisdom, woman's craft, her rage of love
that gave her to serve me strength next divine,
Medea would have made me what I would;
Glaucè but what she could. I schemed amiss
and earned the curses the gods send on fools.
Ruined, ruined! A laughing stock to foes!
No man so mean but he may pity me;
no man so wretched but will keep aloof
lest the curse upon me make him wretcheder.
Ruined!"

                And lo I see him hide his face
like a man who'll weep with passion: but to him
the passion comes not, only slow few tears
of one too weary. And from the great field
where the boys race he hears their jubilant shout
hum through the distance, and he sighs "Ah me!
she might have spared the children, left me them:—
no sons, no sons to stand about me now
and prosper me, and tend me bye and bye
in faltering age, and keep my name on earth
when I shall be departed out of sight."

  And the shout hummed louder
forth: and whirring past
a screaming sea-bird flapped out to the bay,
and listlessly he watched it dip and rise
till it skimmed out of sight, so small a speck
as a mayfly on the brook; and then he said
"Fly forth, fly forth, bird, fly to fierce Medea
where by great Ægeus she sits queening it,
belike a joyful mother of new sons;
tell her she never loved me as she talked,
else had no wrong at my hand shewn so great:
tell her that she breaks oaths more than I broke,

even so much as she seemed to love most—
she who fits fondling in a husband's arms
while I am desolate." And again he said
"My house is perished with me—ruined, ruined!"

   At that he rose and, muttering in his teeth
still "ruined, ruined," slowly paced the sands:
then stood and, gazing on the ragged hulk,
cried "Oh loathed tool of fiends,
that, through all storms
and sundering waters, borest me to Medea,
rot, rot, accursed thing," and petulant
pashed at the side—

               Lo, lo! I see it part!
a tottering spar—it parts, it falls, it strikes!
He is prone on the sand, the blood wells from his brow,
he moans, he speaks, "Medea's prophecy."
See he has fainted.

               Hush, hush! he has lain
with death and silence long: now he wakes up—
"Where is Medea? Let her bind my head."
Hush, hush! A sigh—a breath—He is dead.

             * * * * *

Medea!
What, is it thou? What, thou, this whimpering fool,
this kind meek coward! Sick for pity art thou?
Or did the vision scare thee? Out on me!
do I drivel like a slight disconsolate girl
wailing her love?

No, not one foolish tear
that shamed my cheek welled up for any grief
at his so pitiful lone end. The touch
of ancient memories and the woman's trick
of easy weeping took me unawares:
but grief! Why should I grieve?

And yet for this,
that he is dead. He should still pine and dwine,
hungry for his old lost strong food of life
vanished with me, hungry for children's love,
hungry for me. Ever to think of me—
with love, with hate, what care I? hate is love—
Ever to think and long. Oh it was well!
Yea, my new marriage hope has been achieved:
for he *did* count me happy, picture me
happy with Ægeus; he *did* dream of me
as all to Ægeus that I was to him,
and to him nothing; and *did* yearn for me
and know me lost—we two so far apart
as dead and living, I an envied wife
and he alone and childless. Jason, Jason,
come back to earth; live, live for my revenge.

But lo the man is dead: I am forgotten.
Forgotten; something goes from life in that—
as if oneself had died, when the half self
of one's true living time has slipped away
from reach of memories, has ceased to know
that such a woman is.

A wondrous thing
to be so separate having been so near—
near by hate last and once by so strong love.
Would love have kept us near if he had died

in the good days? Tush, I should have died too:
we should have gone together, hand in hand,
and made dusk Hades glorious each to each.

  Ah me, if then when through the fitful seas
we saw the great rocks glimmer, and the crew
howled "We are lost! lo the Symplegades!"
too late to shun them, if but then some wave,
our secret friend, had dashed us from our course,
sending us to be shivered at the base,
well, well indeed! And yet what say I there?
Ten years together were they not worth cost
of all the anguish? Oh me, how I loved him!
Why did I not die loving him?

* * * * *

                             What thou!
Have the dead no room, or do they drive thee forth
loathing thee near them? Dost thou threaten me?
Why, so I saw thee last, and was not scared:
think not to scare me now; I am no babe
to shiver at an unavailing shade.
Go, go, thou canst not curse me, none will hear:
the gods remember justice. Wrongs! thy wrongs!
the vengeance, ghost! What hast thou to avenge
as I have? Lo, thy meek-eyed Glaucè died,
and thy king-kinsman Creon died: but I,
I live what thou hast made me.

                             Oh smooth adder,
who with fanged kisses changedst my natural blood
to venom in me, say, didst thou not find me
a grave and simple girl in a still home,
learning my spells for pleasant services

or to make sick beds easier? With me went
the sweet sound of friends' voices praising me:
all faces smiled on me, even lifeless things
seemed glad because of me; and I could smile
to every face, to everything, to trees,
to skies and waters, to the passing herds,
to the small thievish sparrows, to the grass
with sunshine through it, to the weed's bold flowers:
for all things glad and harmless seemed my kin,
and all seemed glad and harmless in the world.
Thou cam'st, and from the day thou, finding me
in Hecate's dim grove to cull my herbs,
didst burn my cheeks with kisses hot and strange,
the curse of thee compelled me. Lo I am
The wretch thou say'st; but wherefore? by whose work?
Who, binding me with dreadful marriage oaths
in the midnight temple, led my treacherous flight
from home and father? Whose voice when I turned,
desperate to save thee, on my own young brother,
my so loved brother, whose voice as I smote
nerved me, cried "Brave Medea"? For whose ends
did I decoy the credulous girls, poor fools,
to slay their father? When have I been base,
when cruel, save for thee, until—Man, man,
wilt thou accuse my guilt? Whose is my guilt?
mine or thine, Jason? Oh, soul of my crimes,
how shall I pardon thee for what I am?

Never.   And if, with the poor womanish heart
that for the loving's sake will still love on,
I could let such a past wane as a dream
and turn to thee at waking—turn to thee!
I, put aside like some slight purchased slave
who pleased thee and then tired, still turn to thee!—
yet never, not if thou and I could live

thousands of years and all thy years were pain
and all my years were to behold thy pain,
never could I forgive thee for my boys;
never could I look on this hand of mine
that slew them and not hate thee. Childless thou,
what is thy childlessness to mine? Go, go,
thou foolish angry ghost, what wrongs hast thou?
would I could wrong thee more. Come thou sometimes
and see me happy.

                Dost thou mock at me
with thy cold smiling? Aye, can I not love?
What then? am I not folded round with love,
with a life's whole of love? There doth no thought
come near to Ægeus save what is of me:
am I no happy wife? And I go proud,
and treasure him for noblest of the world:
am I no happy wife?

                Dost mock me still?
My children is it? Are the dead so wise?
Why, who told thee my transport of despair
when from the Sun who willed me not to die
nor creep away, sudden and too late came
the winged swift car that could have saved them, mine,
from thee and from their foes? Tush, 'twas best so;
If they had lived, sometimes thou hadst had hope:
for thou wouldst still have said "I have two sons,"
and dreamed perchance they'd bring thee use at last
and build thy greatness higher: but now, now,
thou hast died shamed and childless, none to keep
thy name and memory fresh upon the earth,
none to make boast of thee "My father did it."

Yea, 'twas best so: my sons, we are avenged.
Thou, mock me not. What if I have ill dreams
to see them loathe me, fly from me in dread,
when I would feed my hungry mouth with kisses?
what if I moan in tossing fever thirsts,
crying for them whom I shall have no more,
here nor among the dead, who never more,
here nor among the dead, will smile to me
with young lips prattling "Mother, mother dear"?
what if I turn sick when the women pass
that lead their boys, and hate a child's young face?
what if—

    Go, go, thou mind'st me of my sons,
and then I hate thee worse; go to thy grave
by which none weeps. I have forgotten thee.

Made in the USA
Columbia, SC
02 December 2024

48133202R00062